Moshe Menasheof

Is it Necessary to Assume the Unconscious?

כתב הוצאה לאור

KTAV Publishing Israel
www.ktav.co.il

Copyright © 2017
Ktav Web Publishing Ltd.
info@ktav.co.il +972-52-4006199
ISBN 978-965-7506-51-6

Is it Necessary to Assume the Unconscious?

Moshe Menasheof

ABSTRACT: Does the unconscious exist? This essay argues that this is not the right question to ask. Rather, what one should ask, and answer, is whether the unconscious is a necessary assumption in order to explain the structure of human episteme. The essay presents an attempt to arrive at the primary foundation of this assumption. The author argues that the primary reason for the need to assume the unconscious was the attempt to deal with the question "why does a person remember a specific content and not others in a particular moment?", or "why did a person have a certain dream and not another?" and that it was this question which led Freud to assume the existence of the unconscious. This assumption is questioned and an alternative is presented. This alternative represents a position which does not assume the unconscious to answer the aforementioned question or explain the entire structure of human episteme.

There is an interesting parallel between the concept of the unconscious and the concept of a UFO. UFO stands for Unidentified Flying Object, but almost everyone who uses it identifies the 'unidentified' as an alien spaceship. Even people who do not believe that creatures from other planets, thousands or millions of light-years away, come to earth, even they use the term UFO as meaning an alien spaceship. They would say, for example, when speaking of Area 51 near Roswell, New-Mexico, that "there can't have really been UFOs there."

In the same way, the unconscious literally means what is not conscious. That is, everything that has been forgotten. However, most people use the term 'unconscious' to mean an inner, hidden world, which affects our thoughts, our decisions and our actions, and that by delving into its depths we can be enriched by new meanings and interpretations. Many refer to the unconscious as a primary strata of the person, a sort of wild, primordial territory that controls its being, without the person knowing or being able to protect himself against it. Some believe that in psychoanalysis the patients can be helped by "bringing to the surface" of their consciousness parts of this terra incognita.

In the same way, just as those who discuss UFOs can discuss spaceships and aliens of different and varied characteristics, some use, instead of the term "unconscious", other terms, such as subconscious or paraconscious, in order to better express this hidden world which affects the person's decision and actions and exists besides, beneath or above the conscious world. However, even this terminology does not change the overall picture in which we discuss something, argue over its existence or lack of, and specifically its different expressions, without truly understanding what is at the basis of assuming this existence.

I intend to show here that the concept of the unconscious is equivalent to that of a UFO, and not to that of alien spaceships coming from far away planets. If one is to use the term 'unconscious' as they use the term UFO, meaning alien spaceships, they should know that they must understand the implications of such a use. That is, there is a need to understand the theoretical foundations of assuming the existence of the unconscious, just as when using the term UFO there is a need to take into account the distance of other planets from earth. There is also a need to take into account the maximum speed that can be reached when travelling this distance and the possibility that these approximations of distance and speeds are merely assumptions valid in our current scientific paradigm (and might be wrong). Therefore, one must first understand what is the basis of the theoretical necessity to assume the existence of the unconscious.

Why is a Person Reminded of a Specific Content in a Specific Moment?

In every moment, a person is reminded of a specific content, intentionally or by free association. The basic question to ask is 'why he is reminded of that specific content, out of infinitely many others?' Why, for example, is a person reminded of his birthday cake falling two years ago, and not of uncountable other instances he can easily remember, or even those he finds it hard to remember?

A similar question should be asked of a person's dreams. Certain content appears in someone's dream. This begs the question – why does she dream specifically those dreams and not others, with other contents?

These are fundamental questions which lead us to take a stance regarding the structure of the human consciousness, in order to try and understand it. In order to do so, we must first define what characterizes the content found in a specific moment in the person's consciousness, and sets them apart from those that are not in consciousness, but can be remembered; and furthermore – what characterizes those contents that a person finds it difficult to remember.

Consciousness as a Hallway Through Which Objects Pass to the Space of the Unconscious

We will describe the world of consciousness using the metaphor of a person standing in a lighted hallway at the entrance to a massive warehouse. Where the person stands there are all kinds of objects, and he can see them passing through the lighted hallway, as if on a conveyor belt. The warehouse is full of a large amount of different objects, which have gone through the hallway during the person's life. It is pitch black in the warehouse, and the person cannot identify anything in it, even if he enters it (assuming he can enter).

The matter we have to discuss is how and when what is recalled to the described person's consciousness is the specific content of his birthday cake falling? Even if we were to say that something in his consciousness hinted at or pointed at this memory, some context which caused it to arise, we are still required to explain how he was able to identify this specific content in the completely dark warehouse – the world of oblivion.

Only a Thing That Has Meaning can Refer to A Thing That Has Meaning.

While in the dark warehouse, the contents cannot be identified. That is, they have no meaning because they are not in consciousness. Only when the content is in consciousness it has meaning for the person, and only a thing that has meaning can refer to another thing that has meaning. There cannot be in one side of the equation, regardless of which side, something meaningless. For example, it cannot be said that the word 'table' points at certain objects of the plethora of objects in the utter darkness. Although it can be assumed that there are tables in the dark warehouse for the world 'table' to mark, the label 'table' cannot be applied to those, nor can they be taken out, since the warehouse is dark and the tables are indistinguishable from the other objects in it.

The question arises, then: how are some contents recalled from the large warehouse, whether intentionally or by free association? If the warehouse is indeed utterly dark, we cannot see what is in it, and therefore, if we plan to recall a certain content, it is impossible to find and take it out, not even by free association. This is because in order to take out a specific content from the warehouse, one associatively connected to a conscious content, we must identify the content in the warehouse [in order to find the associative connection].

The Basic Motive for Assuming the Unconscious

The state of affairs where we assume that the dark warehouse contains objects that cannot be identified when we intend to take out a specific object seems to be a dead-end. Some choose to turn the table, and say that it is not consciousness (or what's in it) that causes a certain content to be taken out from the dark warehouse, but that the object therein have their own energy, like little toys powered by little, battery operated, engines. These toys aspire (are driven) to move towards the exit, to the lighted hallway, and are programmed to do so. Those near the entrance can easily go out, and those pushed to inner departments can hardly come out, and if they do, do so mostly by resembling those nearer the entrance.

That is – since the person's consciousness cannot discover what is in the dark warehouse, it also cannot ascertain which object (content) in the warehouse is linked to its content. It is impossible that a certain content would be recalled out of oblivion, which is the darkness of consciousness, in context of what is in consciousness. One of the ways out of this dead-end is to assume that, like the toys described, the contents in the dark warehouse have an innate ability to come out to the light of consciousness. The assumption that contents have their own energy is the basic foundation for the assumption of the unconscious. On the basis of this assumption we can explain why things we didn't want or didn't mean to be reminded of still arrive in consciousness. However, we will have difficulties explaining how a person can deliberately remember a specific content. To explain this, we must assume some mechanism that can identify the contents of the unconscious. Therefore, for those who assume that the contents are being driven from the subconscious to the conscious, there is no escape from assuming that there is a sub-conscious, a sort of consciousness hidden from the apparent consciousness, in which the contents in the darkness are managed. Under the cover of this sub-conscious, different forces move those contents, connect them, and push them into consciousness. Moreover, even if the contents do not arrive at consciousness, they can influence a person's thoughts, decisions and actions.

Another possibility is to say that this image, of the consciousness as a lit hallway at the entrance to a dark warehouse, does not necessarily accurately present the totality of human consciousness. It is possible that the unconscious is also a part of the consciousness, although differently – the consciousness reigns over the person's entire range of knowledge, and in this range, only what is lit is conscious, and what isn't is in the unconscious. That is – everything is in the dark warehouse, along with a stock-keeper holding a torch, and what is conscious is only what is lit by the torch.

There is essentially no difference between this image and the aforementioned one. Here, to, it must be explained how contents arrive from oblivion to the light. Does the stock-keeper (which represents consciousness, which identifies and gives meaning) determine what will be lit by the torch, or are contents being pushed into the light? In this way, even if we assume that consciousness is the person's entire sphere of awareness, and contains also the contents in oblivion, the general image remains the same – that what is in darkness has no meaning and cannot be identified. That is because the very fact that contents are in oblivion is equivalent to the status of the objects in the dark. That is – the image change in that that consciousness, instead of being the lighted hallway at the entrance to the dark warehouse, is only a small lighted area in an otherwise dark warehouse. Therefore, the reference to the unconscious will not change, and there would still be no answer to the question of how can a person intentionally remember contents related to a specific subject.

Some will say there is a way to identify the contents in the dark. That is, while what is lighted by the torch is conscious and what isn't is unconscious, it is still possible to identify what isn't lighted using infrared goggles, which identifies objects in the dark using the heat they radiate, and in this way identify them and distinguish between contents. According to this description the assumption of the unconscious begs another assumption, of another stock-keeper who wanders around the warehouse with infrared goggles. However, if we keep the same stock-keeper, then in essence we have foregone the explanation according to which contents are being pushed from the unconscious to the conscious, rather than recalled. This description solves the problem and undoes the need for the assumption that the contents are being pushed from the subconscious to the conscious since, by this explanation, they can be recalled by identifying them. Just as on a webpage we can identify, to a certain extent, what is on other pages, using the links to them and what the links tell us. However, we cannot identify all the contents in the other page before we open the link to it.

Does the Unconscious Affect a Person's Actionsand Decisions?

We can agree that whether we assume the existence of the unconscious system or not, the conscious is everything that is in our consciousness at this moment in the present, and is a very small part from the totality of contents a person can remember from the dark warehouse. A very small part, because it is clear that there are orders of magnitude more information in oblivion than in consciousness. However, this image should not be seen as a proof that the unconscious contents have an effect on our thoughts, decisions and actions, and attempting to claim that such an effect exists is far-reaching. That is, it is not enough to determine that the conscious content is only the tip of the iceberg of a person's sphere of contents to assume that the contents in the unconscious affect a person's decision and consciousness.

According to a different argument, these (unconscious) contents can affect our thoughts, decisions and actions even without reaching consciousness. Those who argue that can point to the fact that every decision a person makes and all of her perceptions are related in some why to past knowledge, which is largely unconscious, that is – in oblivion. Just as in the simple example of a man who sees a table and is affected by past knowledge without the content related to this seeing existing in his consciousness. In another example – a person who decides not to confront an abusive manager is affected by his past experiences, even if the relevant contents were not conscious during the decision.

The effect of different contents, conscious or unconscious on a person's thoughts, decision and actions is apparent as suppositions, conscious or unconscious. On the basis of these suppositions he arrives at his conceptions, but this does not mean that unconscious contents, being outside consciousness, can affect what is in consciousness. This effect can be explained only by the way the conscious units of meaning carry layers of information (like links on a webpage). These layers of meaning may be identified only implicitly, and it may even be possible that when they are examined they become conscious. But being in the margin of consciousness, and having no additional units of meaning around their subject, they are instantly forgotten. This enables an explanation of how suppositions the person is not aware of, or cannot point to, indirectly affect her perception.

There are also those who base their argument on the effect of the unconscious by saying that the unconscious contents rise into consciousness independently, ant that the very fact of this possibility can explain the effect they have on our thoughts, decisions and actions, without us being aware of it. They use as evidence contents we suppressed because we didn't "want" to remember, but that still surface in our consciousness, and even find their way into our dreams.

One prominent example of the argument based on the effect of the unconscious on what is in consciousness, without the person meaning to and without being aware of the contents, is the slip of the tongue. These are utterances said unintentionally, especially those that contain certain sexual implications. Slips of the tongue are seen as evidence that the unconscious contents are pushed into the consciousness without the person meaning or wanting them to, and that there is an effect of the unconscious contents, driven by innate energies, on the contents of the consciousness.

However, this phenomenon too can be explained without the need to assume that unconscious contents are driven. That is, without assuming the existence of an unconscious system. In every moment of thought, experience or memory, different contents are being recalled into the conscious, with different relations to the conscious contents; some of them are compatible with the map of data revealed to the person in that moment and some of them are not. But in most cases they are partially compatible, and we improve on their compatibility. One of the ways to explain slips of the tongue is that they are part of the contents that are not compatible with the state of affairs the person is in in that moment. That is, they are contents that are recalled and are not compatible with the subject in our stream of consciousness at the time.

It can also be explained that the slips of the tongue are contents that conform the reality laid out before the person to the different stimuli which convey to her information about this reality. However, they are not compatible with the person's intention in the conversation or thought. That is, they are not part of the main stream of the person's consciousness. These are contents in the margins of the stream of consciousness, who by associative connotations are thickened and find a place in the stream of consciousness, and by that manage to appear, that is to take a central place in the stream of consciousness – in momentary outbursts.

Therefore, the existence of these slips cannot prove any claim regarding the existence of the unconscious or the effect of the unconscious on the conscious. It does not prove that contents arise in consciousness without its control because they have an innate energy. Different contents can be recalled into consciousness with relation to what is conscious, even without the person's intentions. When a man is focused on a specific subject, this subject is in the center of his stream of consciousness, and there is a sort of directing force that navigates the recall of contents related to this subject. This navigation is done in the "sea" of possibilities for associative connections. However, it is possible that during this navigation, other contents will be pulled out, inadvertently and without compatibility to the central subject of the person's stream of consciousness at that moment.

The directing of recalling contents related to a certain subject is lacking in free imagery and absent from dreaming. In these conditions the contents are being recalled by free association – as if the boat sails through the sea of possibilities for associative context, without anyone directing it to anywhere in particular. That is, dreams too can be explained using the supposition that unconscious contents (from oblivion or from the sphere of past knowledge) are being recalled into the conscious with relation to its contents. Therefore, when explaining dreams there is still no necessity to assume that the subconscious contents are being pushed haphazardly, and disguised as unrepressed contents, they succeed in passing through the censoring obstacles.

Does the Unconscious Exist? What is the Meaning of its Existence or Non-Existence?

The question "Does the unconscious exist?" is similar to the question "Do UFOs exist?" the answer to the second question is that there may indeed be objects that this or that person does not recognize, and it may even be that with the existing human knowledge they cannot be identified and explained. But this answer doesn't decide the matter of UFOs if we understand the term to mean alien spaceships coming to earth to visit us or for some other purpose.

Therefore, the first question, that of the existence of the unconscious, is also irrelevant. This question is meaningless since when we talk about the unconscious we do not mean something that has been discovered, but something that has been invented to answer a particular need – that is, the assumption made when trying to explain human psychological phenomena and processes. And if so, then we must ask – is it necessary to assume the unconscious with all of its manifestations, in order to explain the happenings of the human psyche?

Just as some assume that UFOs exist, and as proof show many and varied evidence, so there is evidence for the existence of the unconscious. However, this evidence is nothing but guesswork and conjectures, born out of a belief in the existence of the subconscious. This evidence of the existence of the unconscious come mostly from many years of analysis and other forms of psychotherapy that are based on the assumption of the existence of the unconscious. The therapists point to the many occasions in which, they claim, they have succeeded in aiding patients by resurfacing unconscious content into consciousness.

Of those who believe in the existence of UFOs there are some who assume that UFOs and alien arrive regularly to Earth, abduct humans and animals and experiment on them in their spaceship. They present testimonies by people who claim to have been kidnapped, and even show strange marks on their bodies which they claim can be nothing but the results of alien experimentation. There are also those who claim they communicate with aliens, who might not even have a physical body. They insist they can communicate with the aliens and receive messages which aid in curing diseases and telling the future. Those who hold this belief say that the messages coming from the aliens are meant especially to aid humanity, and that in some cases the aliens' advices have even saved lives. Those who believe in aliens take their existence to be a fact, since they believe they hold evidence of such existence. However, they should be distinguished from those who consider the possibility that aliens exist, but claim there is no evidence they were ever here. We have to distinguish between those who believe in UFOs and those who point to pictures of flying objects as proof of UFOs.

In the light of belief, conjectures are painted as truth, and assumptions seem to be solid facts. However, in actual fact belief is not enough to prove, for example, that photos considered to be pictures of UFO actually do show spaceships coming to earth, carrying intelligent aliens. The same is true for the unconscious – the belief in its existence cannot be considered proof of that existence. It is the belief in the existence of the unconscious which colors the evidence of its existence with the light of a solid truth. Even if there is evidence that assuming its existence can benefit, psychologically, certain people, this evidence do not constitute a justification to this assumption. And we should distinguish between the claim that there are unconscious objects in oblivion, and the claim that these unconscious objects have different effects on the person.

There are various conceptions of the unconsciousness, but they all have in common the principle that the unconscious content is not "turned off", but, while unconscious, affects our thoughts, our decisions and our actions. Each holder of these conceptions present evidence to base his opinion. However, if the discussion is not purely philosophical, in most cases it is played out in the scientific, or more precisely, pseudo-scientific arena – and there we encounter paradigms. In these pseudo-scientific arguments, the unconscious is in fact a discovered, existing entity, which is more than an assumption meant to explain a mental or psychological phenomenon. Treating the unconscious as an assumption which aids in explaining such phenomena is also done while ignoring the current state of knowledge on the subject – we know nothing about psychological processes which have to do with consciousness, and everything we can discuss is conjecture-based.

We realize, therefore, that the very question of the existence of the unconscious is wrong; we should rather ask: which constraints have brought us to assume its existence? In this capacity, we must examine the degree of necessity of this assumption – how well it explains the entirety of phenomena, not only some of them, and at what price. In this way the advantages and disadvantages of this assumption will be revealed.

What is the Price of the Assumption that Contents in Oblivion Have a Self-Drive to Reach Consciousness?

To explain the phenomena that happens in certain situation, such as unconscious contents rising into consciousness, and as a result the slips of the tongue (especially those containing sexual innuendos), many psychotherapists assume that the unconscious content have an inherent energy, or that different forces, such as the drive for self-gratification,[1] move such contents and push them into consciousness. We should note that those slips of the tongue are shown as evidence proving the existence of the unconscious, when the assumption of the unconscious itself is based on these events. In other words – the slips of the tongue are explained based on the assumption of the unconscious, and are also presented as support for that very same assumption, that the unconscious exists.

Even if we ignore this problem of circular thinking, assuming the existence of the unconscious makes it difficult to explain normal cognitive processes, such as seeing a table, or remembering the table a person has seen yesterday. This is because if the contents in oblivion, the unconscious contents, have a drive of their own which propels them into consciousness, how can we explain the fact that they do not flood the consciousness of the person upon arriving to it, but only arise following certain circumstances? To answer this

---

[1]. The "ego" (self) the "Super-ego" (over-self), the "Id" (the natural drives, or the born self, guided by drives of sex and violence in order to produce enjoyment) and the "Libido" (the sexual component of the id).

question we must assume that there is a division of the unconscious to areas of sub-conscious and near-conscious, and that there are passages through them, manned by guards who censor unwanted content, prevent it from reaching consciousness, and enable only the contents they wish to arrive at consciousness to do so. This explains that when, for example, a person sees a table, the guards allow the content of seeing a table to reach consciousness. This replaces the explanation that a certain optical stimuli causes the information about seeing a table to be recalled or that a person remembers in a specific context, the table he has seen in a store the day before.

If the unconscious is assumed to exist, than the fact of the slip of the tongue happening means a systematic failure, since the guards failed to do their duty. While such systematic failures can be considered evidence for the existence of the system, such an assumption on the basis of pointing to failures alone is invalid, especially when an explanation can be given accounting for situations when different contents arrive at consciousness following drives, and against a person's will to repress them and keep them from arriving there.

The price we pay is that while we grasp the examples of slips of the tongues and dreams, which we can consider abnormal and reasonably explain, we lose the basic explanation for the question – why are things usually (if not always) remembered in context of what is already in consciousness. That is, assuming the unconscious may explain how a person can, by a slip of the tongue, remember what he has repressed, but it fails to explain the way a person sees and deliberately remembers what serves his functioning.

When we try to explain the abnormalities (such as slips of the tongue), we mustn't forget that the explanation should also explain normal events (such as remembering a table I have seen yesterday). At times it seems that explaining these abnormalities is projected and forced upon the regular events.

Therefore, the explanation according to which in our everyday experiences and memories contents are being pushed and driven into our consciousness in a random fashion is complicated and necessitates assuming different types of drives, which may explain the abnormal, but not necessarily the every-day. The unconscious contents can be explained to be recalled according to the context of contents in our consciousness. This recalling is adapted to serve our functioning in the atmosphere in which we live. However, there are quite a few cases where it seems that it is different emotions which are the catalysts to this passage of contents to the lit area of consciousness, and now is the time to discuss them.

Is it Emotions that Drives Contents from the Unconscious into Consciousness?

There are also many occasions when we have thoughts we do not want to think. That is the case, for example, with a man angry at a woman he loves and has left him. He understands the relationship is over and cannot return to what it was, but it seems that his emotions keep driving him to continually dwell on the subject. Even if he tries to stop them, he cannot. Are emotions, therefore, the drives who motivate the contents to come into consciousness time and again?

To say that emotions, such as anger, disappointment or love, push certain contents to consciousness over and again, we must assume that emotions have a conscious ability through which they identify these contents and pick them out from the rest. For that, the contents must be meaningful for this emotional sub-consciousness. In the model of the dark warehouse and lit hallway, the warehouse is supposed to have lit areas – as if others than the stock-keeper are walking inside with their own torches. That is – if we assume that emotions push contents from the sub-conscious to the conscious, we must assume that in, or besides, the person's consciousness there are other 'consciousnesses'.

To the content of a thought which is related to emotion, when it is in the darkness of oblivion, there is and cannot be any force.

To have the force to drive, there must be contents which the person identifies, and raise in him an emotion which can catalyze the preoccupation with contents surrounding the objects which caused the emotion. Only when these conditions are met, is it possible to assume that the objects in the dark area have a driving force. And even then, in order for some contents which are related to what raises the emotion to be pushed from the unconscious to the conscious, there is a need to recognize these contents from the others, and therefore assume the existence of another consciousness. And since the contents in the dark are not meaningful, it is impossible to attribute to the content or the thought in the dark an independent driving force. In our model, we have to explain how certain object appear again and again in the lit hallway. That is – how contents pass from the unconscious to the conscious, at times despite the person's inclination (will and intention) to avoid them doing so.

These situation, where emotions seem to drive the contents related to it into consciousness can be explained without assuming the unconscious, using a system of contexts and associations between certain contents. This system brings about the recall of certain contents from the darkness of the unconscious into the conscious, even if the person is trying to prevent himself from doing so. One of the reasons for the repeated recall of contents related to a certain matter, which is the object of the emotion, is that by the very attempt of the person to stop thinking about a certain topic, she inadvertently deals with it, and with its related contents, all the more. And then these contents pull from the world of oblivion more contents related to them.

Furthermore, it should be mentioned that a person's emotion is in itself a kind of force which directs thinking. The content in consciousness is the cause of emotion, and the emotions awaken as a reaction to considering the contents in certain framework, or in a certain state of being. Just as a person has perceptual abilities in the dimension of time and the dimension of space, so he can attribute an emotion to a certain content. The emotion has various effects on the person. For example, it causes certain compounds to be secreted in the body, to prompt him to fight or flight, all according to the general purpose of maintaining his functioning and insuring his survival in his environment.

It is not the information itself which holds a certain emotion, but the emotion is created as a result of a person's relation to the content. The relation is possible only when the person identifies the content and is conscious of it, and then he applies his emotional relation to it. That is, the person applies emotion to certain contents, and as a result enters into a certain emotional setting. Applying the emotional relation to the content-based relation is done using a similar mechanism to that which enables a person to comprehend time and space data and apply emotions, proportions and dimensions to them, and by that understand, for example, that a car seems small because it is distant from him, or that a table is square even though it seems as a trapeze.

Emotional excitement as prompting – for example when he is angry, afraid or in love, is only true when the emotional state arises in the present time, when this relation is part of the person's experience. As any other experience, the meanings of the emotions as perceived in the present, will be, in the future, part of the person's past knowledge. Therefore, the information regarding the emotion and emotional state itself is stored in the world of past knowledge, and can be remembered just as any other information.

In this manner, a person may be, for example, angry or afraid because of his relation to a content or a cluster of contents on a certain subject. This person can also perceive himself as angry or afraid, and this information can be recalled in the future just like any other memory. That is, the memory of the anger is in itself a content or information just as any other content recalled into consciousness.

The catalyst for being reminded of contents related to the subject of emotion is mainly the fact that the emotion serves as a context, just like space-time is a context according to which contents are being recalled from oblivion. That is, the more emotionally excited a person is, the richer his contexts are, and so the probability to be reminded of these contents increases.

Human Consciousness can be Explained without Assuming the Unconscious

As can be understood from the explanations presented so far, the person's cognitive processes, including perception, memory and dreaming, can be described without needing to assume the unconscious system and its appendices, such as another consciousness, drives, acting in the same consciousness and obstacles meant to filter the unwanted contents from coming into consciousness, which must all be assumed if the unconscious is assumed. This explanation is consistent with everyday normal processes as well as with abnormal cases in which it seems that the contents of subconscious are being pushed into consciousness.

The discussion thus far has been based on the presumption that contents are indifferent, and receive their meaning only in the light of consciousness, and that only lighted (conscious) contents have meaning for the person. It this manner, what is in oblivion (the unconscious) has no meaning for the person, because she cannot identify it. The contents in the world of past knowledge – those in oblivion or in darkness – are being recalled into consciousness using the context which links what is in consciousness with these contents in oblivion. That is, what is in oblivion is the factor in relation to which contents from the world of oblivion – the dark warehouse in the model – are recalled. On the basis of this presumption, and according to the process pictured here, various problems relating to consciousness can be dealt with and explained. Here are some examples of these problems:

i) **A person is reminded of a table he has seen the day before** – the person is reminded of this specific content in this moment, and not countless other contents he could have been reminded of, because it is this content which is recalled to his consciousness in some context – intentionally or associatively and by chance. Furthermore, according to the aforementioned presumption, and based on the described process, sensuous experiences, such as seeing the table, can be explained in the context of the primal sensuous meaning created by a physical stimulus. This meaning applies when a pattern with information regarding seeing a table is being recalled from the world of past knowledge. The information is processed, and after being located in the present time-space, the person sees a table. Another question arises here – how can a person easily recall certain contents but has difficulties recalling others. As an answer we might point out that owing to a lack of connections to such contents they are less available, and the probability of being recalled into consciousness is being created mostly according to their associations to contents in the person's consciousness.

ii) **An emotional person cannot help being occupied by the object of his emotion** – the thoughts of an angry person, for example, revolve around the object of his anger, even if he doesn't want them to. This means that sometimes a feeling is created that contents which have to do with emotion has a force to move themselves to consciousness, as if an engine is driving them towards it – towards the lighted hallway. However, this is a false impression. The emotion is a powerful context in connection with which more and more contents are recalled, and so a sort of directing by the emotion is created, instead of by the person's logic (intended force), or in parallel with it. Moreover, while relating to the emotion connections are formed, which increase more and more the probability of these contents to be recalled to consciousness. The impression that contents are being driven by emotion to the conscious is formed by the contents relating to a certain subject flashing in memory and increasing the amount of connections. This increases the probability that such contents will be recalled to consciousness, and in effect create a positive feedback loop. This process of a vicious cycle is expressed in situations in which the person is angry and tries to stop thinking about the subject of his anger, to stop "tripping" over it. But he cannot stop thinking about it, and in his consciousness finds himself, over and over, preoccupied with contents relating to the object of his anger.

iii) **A person's slip of the tongue** – a slip of the tongue occurs when a person says words without intending to say them, and does so because the contents in the background of those words were in the outskirts of his consciousness, along with other contents. All this, when it is possible that some of these contents were pushed into oblivion owing to a depletion of connection to them along the years, and in the slip of the tongue they find a way to appear. It is possible, for example, that a man stands in front of a woman, discussing global warming with her while his eyes focus on her appearance, which he finds attractive and sexy. As part of his speech he lets slip a word which has to do with his relation to the woman's appearance, and not to the discussion of global warming. Here, too, there is no need to assume anything beyond these presumptions, according to which only that which is in consciousness has meaning, and those contents in oblivion (the unconscious), as long as they are in oblivion, has no meaning. It can be explained that in that moment, in the man's stream of consciousness, there were contents related to the topic of conversation, but also to the appearance of the woman, and to sounds and discussions heard in the room. In every moment another subject has been prominent in the center of the stream of consciousness such as, for example, the sounds of laughter of other people in the room or the sounds of a waiter passing by them, holding a tray of drinks. All of these contents have been recalled in context with the sensuous stimuli created in the man and what was in his consciousness and flooded it, causing him to momentarily lose his train of thought and say things which are considered a slip of the tongue. That is, even in slips of the tongue in which a person says something he may not have meant to say in the situation where he is, he says it owing to these contents or words being recalled by the connections of contents in his consciousness which connect to certain contents in oblivion (the unconscious) by association.

iv) **A person dreams certain contents, and not others** – during sleep, the ability to think is inactive, and therefore the intention in recalling contents from past knowledge is lacking, and they are recalled in a random-associative context according to what is in consciousness. Therefore, the contents of the dreams are confused and random owing to the release from the ability to think and the force of intention, it is possible that in sleep a person will dream content he could not remember waking up, and so, the lack of the ability to think also explains the dream's vividness. Repressed contents, therefore, can arise in consciousness, while awake or when sleeping, according to the presumption that the contents in oblivion are being recalled to consciousness in the context of the contents in consciousness

Why Freud Still had to Assume the Existence of the Unconscious

Sigmund Freud, Painted by: Ronny Someck

It can be assumed that Sigmund Freud, in building his general theory, was required to find a solution to this basic issue: why in certain moments a person remembers specific contents and not others. He too was faced with the difficulty of explaining how is it possible to recall from oblivion a certain content which has no meaning because it is unrecognizable. It is possible that because of the impossibility of identifying contents in the darkness of consciousness (in the model – the impossibility of identifying the object in the dark warehouse) he chose the explanation that the contents in the darkness have an inherent drive to come out to consciousness (in the model – the objects have a drive which pushes them into the lit hallway). For him, this is a fitting explanation especially to the phenomenon of repressed contents which sneak into consciousness in the slips of the tongue and in dreams. This explanation by Freud fitted well in the therapeutic structure he had built and founded, and after its success, the existence of the unconscious turned from an assumption to a fact.

In allegory – Freud pointed to an unidentified flying object, termed it a UFO and fixed the meaning of this term as an alien spaceship. His discussion of the concept of the unconscious was done with tremendous literary talent and ingenious persuasive ability, which have fixed this term in the public's consciousness and rooted it in different areas of life so successfully that it still resonates through the generations after him. Freud was so successful in making the concept of the unconscious into part of the culture that it is almost never referred to as a collection of things in oblivion. In the same way the concept of UFO was fixed, so instead of referring to it as an object we know nothing about, we see it as an object we know a lot about – we know it is a spaceship of intelligent creatures that have arrived to earth from distant planets and so on. The same happened with the concept of the unconscious, after being fixed successfully by Freud; we recognize its drives, which drive its contents to the conscious and in that affect our thoughts, our decisions and our actions, or it sneaks out once in a while into consciousness – mainly in slips of the tongue and dreams.

Ever since Freud fixed the concept of the unconscious, those who deal with it argue mostly about the question of what characterizes it, just as asking what kind of aliens and spaceship are discussed. Regarding the unconscious, there are arguments about the existence of different variations of it, and even those who oppose Freud, claiming that the unconscious does not exist, use this term as Freud has fixed it. That is – Freud saw it fit to assume the existence of the unconscious, in the meaning that non-conscious contents have a self-drive to arrive at consciousness. His aim in this assumption was to answer the fundamental question – "why do we remember this content and not another?" in order to explain the processes of human cognition as a whole. He did it with such talent that researchers in the field of psychology, and even in other fields such as literature and arts, have been misled by him.

One of the things which strengthened Freud's position and even fixed it was the fact that his method is being applied in psychoanalytic therapy. According to the basic theory of such treatments, if we can identify what has been repressed by a person years ago, then it will be possible to aid him in overcoming problems coming from such repression. However, even if it seems that there are quite a few patients who claim such therapy has helped them, it still does not mean that there is truth in the assumption that if you can surface in a person's memory what has been repressed and forgotten, then he will be cured and released of the sediments the repression has left. But even if this assumption is true, it still does not mean that the assumption of the unconscious is necessary. The process of healing can be explained by that that when a person finally understand what it is he was repressing, and now, after years have gone by, he sees it in the right perspective, the influence of the formerly repressed content decreases and the anxiety of it weakens.

Freud's assumption is that there is some correlation between the person's personal drives. For example, if someone satisfies his sexual needs, then his aggression and pursuit of honor and career advancement declines, and vice-versa. From what has been said thus far we can deduce that this assumption can be an interesting philosophical insight, but can also be nothing but a phrase or a claim with the same validity of astrology or similar fields of fortune telling and mysticism, which also use, at times, a seemingly scientific language. Phrases and aphorisms from such fields lead the person to think that if he believes, what he believes will come true and so, for him, his belief becomes a proven truth.

It turns out then, that from the theoretical possibilities Freud has chosen the one according to which the contents in the darkness of consciousness have a force which drives them to consciousness. It is possible that this choice stems from his inability to explain how objects can be recalled from the dark warehouse. In any case, his assumption is theoretical-philosophical – obviously, it is not necessarily true, and we definitely cannot view its conclusion as having scientific validity.

In conclusion, in every instance there is in the consciousness of the person a certain amount of content, and all the rest is in oblivion. Among the contents in oblivion, there are those who can be remembered, those who the person finds it difficult to remember and even those he cannot remember now, but will be able to in other circumstances. The contents in oblivion – in the dark warehouse of past knowledge, are meaningless, and cannot be identified or distinguished from one another. This fact begs the question of how it is that from the many contents in the dark warehouse, a person is reminded of a specific content at a specific moment. The meaning of the assumption of the existence of the unconscious is that the objects in the dark warehouse are as toys with an automatic mechanism, set at all times to advance towards the hallway. This assumption leads to another assumption, that of the existence of the subconscious, and even makes it hard to explain the everyday situations in which a person, intentionally or in a certain context, remembers a content he wishes to remember. That is, the "price" of this assumption is high.

So, as we should distinguish between a UFO as an unidentified flying object and a UFO as an alien spaceship coming from distant planets, we have to distinguish between using the term unconscious when we mean contents that are not conscious (or are in oblivion) and using the term to mark a system whose contents are unknown, have their own force which drives them to the conscious (to reach consciousness). We can assume that the source of this assumption or claim is in the attempt to answer the question of how the contents arrive at consciousness (intently or associatively) when it cannot identify them. This assumption leads to the explanation according to which they emerge on their own. That is, the explanation to the way a person remembers things is that she doesn't remember them in the meaning that in a certain context she recalls them from the world of oblivion, but that they cause memory by surfacing to consciousness themselves. This explanation has a significant price, because it requires the assumption of another consciousness, of a system such as sub-conscious and near-conscious, of the divide between these system and the conscious and of the censoring of the passage between them.

In contrast, the explanation which does not assume the existence of the unconscious is deserving, or at least not less deserving than the explanation which assumes the existence of the unconscious. The explanation which does not assume the existence of the unconscious clarifies not only a sector or a certain kind of phenomena (such as the phenomenon of repressed contents rising into awareness without the person meaning them, both while awake and when dreaming), but all kinds of perception and memory, including the dreams and states in which the person is under the influence of his emotions. Therefore I believe that the explanation that answers the different issues in the fields of consciousness without assuming the existence of an entity which cannot be proven – should be preferred.